OWLS

Owls
Copyright © 2013 Evans Mitchell Books

Text and photography copyright
© 2013 David Tipling & Jari Peltomäki

David Tipling and Jari Peltomäki
have asserted their rights to be identified as
the authors and photographers of this work
in accordance with Section 77 of the
Copyright, Designs and Patents Act 1988.

First published in the
United Kingdom in 2013 by
Evans Mitchell Books
130 City Road, London EC1V 2NW
United Kingdom
www.embooks.co.uk

Design by
Darren Westlake
TU ink Ltd, London
www.tuink.co.uk

British Library Cataloguing in Publication Data.
A CIP record of this book is available
on request from the British Library.

ISBN: 978-1-901268-62-1

Printed in Spain by GZ Printek

OWLS

DAVID TIPLING & JARI PELTOMÄKI

Evans Mitchell Books

Contents

Introduction

Owls command attention, as the quintessential emblems of darkness. They evoke strong cultural responses, partly because their mysterious lives seem so strange and fascinating to us. Their allure stems partly from them being active mostly at night, but it is also this nocturnal lifestyle that has led to all those sinister associations of owls and their pervasive connections to death and disaster. In Europe this fearful response has now largely been replaced by one of respect, and by feelings of wonder, as we come to learn so much more about their genuine natural history.

Previous page: Hunting great grey owl.

Above: A fluffy ural owl not long out of the nest starts to explore its surroundings.

Left: A female snowy owl hunts during an Arctic summer night.

9

While these folkloric responses might be fascinating, the actual study and photographing of real owls have allowed us to look through a clear window into their secret worlds. Between us we have spent thousands of hours in the wilds and maintained long vigils in cramped hides, or waited in hedgerows, knee-deep in frigid snow fields, sometimes with no results at all to show for it, or at best, for only fleeting opportunities. Photographing owls is a major challenge, but the sight of a barn owl floating moth-like over a meadow on a golden dawn or of a great grey owl plunging into snow after prey brings with it an adrenalin-pumping sense of fulfillment that makes the long wait and the discomfort all tolerable.

This book recounts some of our most memorable experiences as we stood and watched and hoped, over the years, to capture a little more about the private lives of the 12 owl species in northern Europe.

Right: A barn owl stoops on a vole in an english meadow.

10

Silent hunters

On a moonless night in May 1937 a tawny owl sunk a claw deep into Eric Hosking's eye. This celebrated English bird photographer had returned to check on his hide overlooking the owl's nest. He had no chance to avoid the attack because the bird made its deadly approach in total silence. Hosking actually lost that left eye and the story was covered widely in the press but, far from being the disaster one might have thought, it catapulted Hosking to national stardom.

The tale is a perfect illustration of the deadly prowess of owls in conditions of almost complete darkness. Yet in some ways, even more extraordinary is the owls' sense of hearing. This ability is especially impressive in nocturnal species, such as the tawny and Tengmalm's (boreal) owl, and is made possible by an asymmetrical arrangement of the birds' ears (on each side of the head one ear is slightly higher than the other). The sound of a rustling mouse reaches one ear a fraction quicker than it does the other, allowing the bird to fix the source of any noise with exceptional accuracy.

Previous page: A great grey owl can hear a rodent moving below a deep layer of snow and strike with deadly accuracy.

Above: Both the tawny owl pictured and ural owl have a reputation for attacking humans when they fear their nests or young are threatened.

Opposite: The facial disc as evident on this Tengmalm's owl helps funnel sound to its ears.

Left: A barn owl lingers on a gravestone before flying up to feed its chicks at a nest in a church tower.

Below: Northern hawk owl.

Sounds are collected and funneled to the owl's ears by the bird's facial disc, a concave arrangement of feathers across the front of the owl's head. This configuration functions in much the same way as our hands when we cup them behind our ears to try to hear a distant noise.

During scientific experiments some species have been proven to be ten times more sensitive to sound than humans, so that the tiniest peep made by a rodent can be its death sentence. Barn owls have the ability to locate and catch prey using only their ears while hunting in the dark.

This uncanny sensitivity can also be used during daylight hours, not least by great grey owls that can detect sounds muffled below a deep layer of snow, the bird diving right through this to grab the rodents below.

Jari Peltomäki observes:

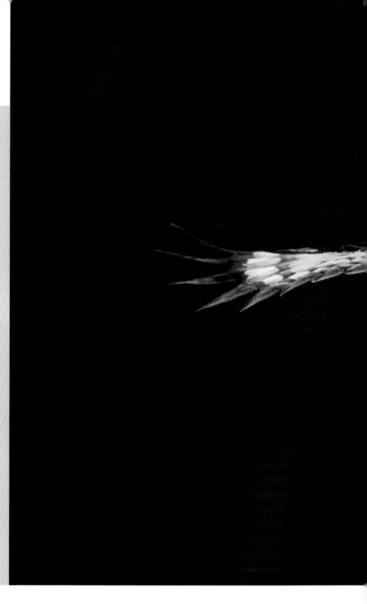

"In some years when there are not many voles available, the owls can be starving and then they readily accept offered dead mice. However, this doesn't happen every year and the owls can come to hunt in the open in daylight, especially, for example, if there are plenty of voles in a certain field.

A great grey owl will fly over an area where there are voles and briefly hover. When it locates its prey the owl dives head first, then just before hitting the snow, will turn its legs so they strike the snow first. Great grey owls can spend some time sitting in snow – especially if they miss the vole, then they will try to find it by feeling about with their feet. If they have missed with the dive they are rarely successful. However, they are very efficient vole hunters.

There are years when great grey owls die of starvation due to the lack of food or because the snow has too hard a crust which they cannot break through. I am convinced that I have saved many great grey owls' lives by feeding them during these harsh winters."

Above, right: Great grey owl.

Below: A Eurasian pygmy owl plunges into the snow in pursuit of a rodent.

Opposite: A northern hawk owl swoops down on to an unsuspecting rodent under the snow.

18

Above: The eye of a long-eared owl.

Left: Owls cannot see in absolute darkness but in low light they can see far better than humans. This is a close-up of a short-eared owl's eye.

For many northern species, like the great grey owl, hunting involves both auditory signals and visual cues. It is a myth that owls can see in absolute darkness, they cannot, but their eyes in low light are far more sensitive than our own.

An owl's eye is shaped more like a tube as opposed to the ball of a human eye. It is fused to the skull by sclerotic rings that prevent it rolling and moving in its socket as our own eyes can. So to look left or right an owl moves its head, some species such as the long-eared owl being able to rotate it through an impressive 270 degrees.

In animals with forward-facing eyes, where the image produced in each eye overlaps with the other, the resulting effect is known as binocular vision. It allows distances to be judged more accurately. You will often see an owl bob or weave his head. This is to gain depth perception and, in effect, improve its three-dimensional view.

While most birds of prey have eyes designed for acuity, owls' eyes lack visual sharpness but they have evolved to give the birds maximum sensitivity in low light. An owl can make out shape and movement easily at dusk or after dark, but the sharpness and overall quality of the image it sees will be relatively poor with little colour information. This ability to see in low light is made possible by having very large eyes relative to their size; indeed, many species have eyeballs bigger and heavier than a human's.

Owls have a large pupil, the part of the eye that determines how much light is let in to reach the retina. This can be closed as small as needed for seeing in bright light but can open to allow the maximum amount of light into the eye in low light. The retina which captures this light is packed with photoreceptors. There are two types of these, rods and cones, and the latter serve us well in defining colour. Owls' eyes are packed with rods but with far fewer cones. It is the rods that are light sensitive and provide the ability to see well in low light. However that is not to say owls have no colour vision. They have enough cones in the retina to differentiate colour in good daylight. Studies have shown this ability varies within species but is better in those that hunt a lot in daylight, such as the starling-sized Eurasian pygmy owl.

Right: A great grey owl is silhouetted against the moon.

Opposite: The Eurasian pygmy owls reputation as a fierce hunter is equalled by his look.

A male snowy owl returns to its nest on the arctic tundra clutching a long-tailed skua chick.

Handle an owl and you might be surprised to find how light it is compared to its size. Indeed many species seem to be nothing but feathers. That low body weight combined with relatively long, broad wings, which are particularly a feature of the larger owl species, gives the birds their buoyant flight. Technically this is known as a low wing-loading. Couple this with very soft flight feathers and you have a bird that makes no noise as it flies. When it sails through the air it

does not need to flap vigorously but can float moth-like and proceed very slowly, hovering with ease. This soundless flight not only helps owls with the element of surprise, since their prey never hear the birds approaching, but it also allows them to listen for prey as they move.

Watching the moth-like passage of a hunting barn owl can be bewitching and there is perhaps no better place to see this in daylight than on the North Norfolk coast.

“I arrived long before sunrise at my favourite meadow for photographing barn owls. It had been a cold shower-laden night but now the sky had cleared, and the moon shone brightly. I wanted to be in position as the sun rose, that magical three or four minutes when the Earth appears as if on fire, a moment when I hoped an owl would be within range. Standing in the lee of a hedge I peered out on to the North Sea. The light was racing across the ground towards my small field and now, as visibility improved, I could see two owls quartering distantly. Slowly they came closer and, as if on cue, while the sun rose, an owl hovered above a line of reeds just a few metres away, golden in the pristine light of an April dawn.”

Not all owls hunt by the same method, but will use a combination of active hunting or wait and see, viewing an area from a tree top or some tucked-away perch. The northern hawk owl is a formidable hunter and a species that hunts in various ways. Hawk owls are most often encountered perched on tree tops, usually spruce, from where they scan for favoured prey – mice and the northern owls' staple, the vole. In Finnish the hawk owl is called *hiiripöllö*, which translates as 'mouse owl'. This name suits it pretty well, since over 95 per cent of a hawk owl's diet in summer is small rodents. This species has remarkable eyesight and can spot a vole running across snow from a mile away. A hawk owl will hover over a meadow listening for voles, but the species is built more for speed and lightening strikes made from tree-top perches.

Previous page: Barn owl.

Opposite and left: While northern hawk owls prefer to wait and watch, as left, they will hover to help locate their prey.

Above: Barn owls commonly quarter a meadow, actively hunting for their prey, but they will also watch from a perch too.

David Tipling observes:

" A few winters ago we visited a farm in central Finland where a hawk owl had taken up residence. Each morning the owner would go around her farm buildings collecting dead mice from her traps and would throw these to the hawk owl that always perched at the top of a spruce by her farmhouse. The owl took the mice off into the forest, often collecting more than it could eat each day. These were being stored in clefts and cracks in trees, so that, in effect, the neighbouring trees had become its larder. The hawk owl became very tame and would take mice from the owner's outstretched hand. Photographers heard about these performances and visited in droves. Not to miss a money-making opportunity, the farm owner began to charge each photographer €15 for three mice that she placed in the snow. These enabled spectacular action shots to be taken and hundreds of people visited the farm that winter.

Hawk owls fly astonishingly fast and so capturing a sharp image such as this can be a challenge. However they will always fly into the wind. So by waiting upwind in line with where the owl would swoop to collect its prey and by pre-focussing I was able to start firing the cameras shutter as the bird came into view through my viewfinder resulting in this image."

Hawk owls will readily take birds as part of their diet, but the fiercest bird-catcher in years when vole populations are low is the diminutive Eurasian pygmy owl. They can hunt birds in swift flight but will readily raid tree-hole nest sites and seize young and adults from nest boxes.

Pygmy owls are not the only species to take avian prey; indeed, they need to be careful they

are not preyed upon themselves. Owls readily prey on other owls, this behaviour being known as 'intraguild predation'. The Eurasian eagle owl is a voracious predator and will take

Above: Short-eared owls are most likely to hunt during daylight.

any raptor within its territory, as witnessed in Belgium a few years ago:

David Tipling observes:

" As dusk enveloped the surrounding forest, the eagle owl we were watching on the quarry face disappeared into the trees. Seconds after it had glided through the pine canopy I heard a blood-curdling screech and much commotion. Minutes later it re-appeared carrying a large bird in its talons. Once back on the cliff ledge it was clear it had caught a female northern sparrowhawk. "

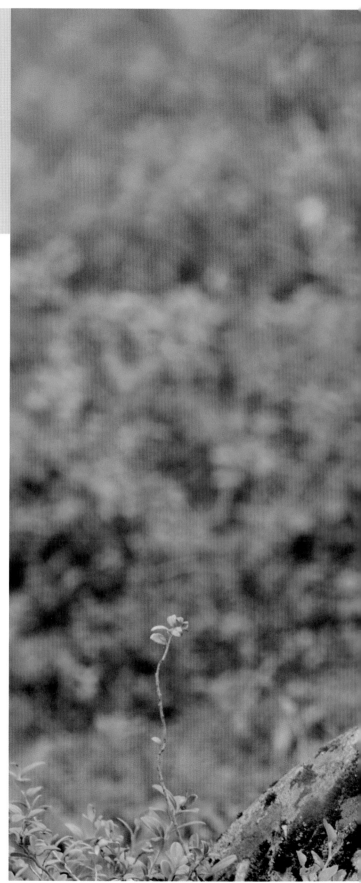

Above: The eagle owl's large eyes gives this fierce hunter exceptional vision in the dark.

Right: This young eagle owl will in a few days be able to fly but will still be reliant on it's parents for another three to four months until they chase it from their territory.

This predation is by no means unusual. Eurasian eagle owls, like other owl species, will eliminate competition from their territories if they perceive it to be a threat to their survival and ability to rear a family. Equally other birds of prey will prey on owls. Golden Eagles have been recorded taking Eurasian eagle owls, while forest-dwelling species like northern goshawks will prey on birds such as Tengmalm's and Eurasian pygmy owls.

Above & opposite: Tengmalm's owls are only active at night, so during the day to avoid predation by other owls and raptors such as goshawks, they hide away. But if you find a hole suited to a breeding Tengmalm's owl and scratch the trunk to mimic a potential predator, you might get a surprise when an owl appears at the hole to give you a stare.

Kleptoparasitism is the name given to the habit of stealing prey that was initially captured by another bird or animal. Some owl species are common victims of this behaviour. In Norfolk, where barn owls hunt frequently during daylight, Eurasian kestrels have become common thieves of their prey. Typically if a barn owl is quartering a meadow the kestrel will sit atop a large tree and watch intently. If a barn owl hunts successfully the kestrel will immediately attack. These assaults are most successful during the breeding season, when the owl has to carry the prey back to its nest and is raided in mid flight.

Above & right: Barn owls are normally nocturnal, but in Britain and particularly in eastern England, this species can be seen hunting during the day, especially in late winter and when feeding young in summer.

Above & left: A rare breeding species in europe, the snowy owl roams across the remote landscapes of the far north.

Above: A northern hawk owl merges perfectly against the tree trunk as he sits tight against his nest hole.

Right: A northern hawk owl watching for prey.

Above: A tawny owl peers through autumn colour from a daytime roost in a beech tree.

Left: A short-eared owl clutching a vole, swoops into a nest hidden in a Finnish meadow.

Breeding

Before a commitment to breed is made an owl pair needs to be confident there is good prey availability. For sedentary species, such as little and barn owls that breed in more southerly latitudes, this is less of an issue, because food availability is more stable, if still often cyclical. In northern latitudes vole and lemming populations have a three-to-five-year cycle of abundance with populations peaking and then crashing. There is much debate over what drives these cycles. Factors may include the amount of winter snow cover, food availability and predator pressure on the population. Nomadic species such as great grey and hawk owls need to react to these population fluctuations and so move in response. A location that supports breeding owls one year may be devoid of them the next if the vole or lemming population has crashed.

Previous page: Great grey owls often take over large stick nests used by other birds including goshawks.

Above & opposite: Bank and field voles, and in more northerly latitudes, lemmings, are a favoured prey of northern hawk owls in summer.

Above & opposite: The plumage of young northern hawk owls just out of the nest, blends in well with the grey shades of lichen-covered branches and bark. This helps the chick, once out of the nest, to remain relatively unobtrusive protecting from predation. Chicks however, can make noisy demands on their parents when bringing in food, such as here.

The annual variability in abundance of breeding northern hawk owls in Finland illustrates this well. During good vole years there can be up to 6,000 breeding pairs and in bad vole years just a few. They may fly thousands of kilometres to find an area with a plentiful food supply.

The snowy owl is another nomad that nests on the Arctic tundra. During a good lemming year a pair may raise a dozen or more young, catching in excess of 2,000 lemmings. In years when snowy owls are unable to locate a region with abundant food they may not breed, or will attempt to rear a few chicks and may have to prey on birds, with wader chicks and ducklings being common targets.

A good example of how an individual owl will move in response to prey availability is illustrated by the story of a leucistic great grey owl in Finland Because of her blonde appearance she soon became affectionately known as Linda after a famous and sexy Finnish violinist, Linda Brava.

Linda was first seen in 1994 at Vesanto in central Finland. By 1995 she had moved 170 kilometres north to Kajaani. She then disappeared until in March 1998 one of the authors found her 200 kilometres north west of Kajaani at the coastal village of Liminka. Jari recalls that day...

Opposite & left: Linda,
the leucistic great grey owl,
became an avian celebrity.

Jari Peltomäki observes:

"In 1998 I was photographing a wintering snowy owl in fields near Oulu. One day I went back to these fields and could not find the owl. So I searched around with my binoculars when I noticed a white owl on the dark forest edge around one kilometre away. I was wondering what the snowy owl was doing on the edge of the forest, because normally it perched on the barn roofs in the middle of the fields.

I went closer and was very surprised to see it was actually an almost white great grey owl! I was very lucky that evening, since the full moon was rising early, allowing me to photograph this beautiful owl with the moon behind.

I was lucky to find Linda again in the summer of 2000. This time she was nesting in a forest with a normal-coloured male, 130 kilometres east of where I found her in 1998. I spent only one day with her on that occasion, but I managed to get some more images. The pair produced three normal-coloured great grey owl youngsters.

In the winter of 2003 I found her again, 140 kilometres to the north, she was starving. I was able to feed her dead mice – she was so hungry that she ate ten mice that day. I went back for several days to feed her, then when she was fit enough, she left the area as it was time for her to go back in to the forest to breed. However, I believe my supplementary feeding saved her life.

I no longer dream of finding her again; too much time has passed, but it is always possible that another leucistic great grey owl will appear one day."

Above: By dissecting owl pellets such as this one produced by a snowy owl, and looking at the bones, feather and fur, we can identify the animals they have eaten.

Left: A male snowy owl arrives at the nest with prey which is grabbed by the female (left) as their hungry chicks look on.

Linda lived for over nine years and illustrates how nomadic species will move in response to prey availability.

Courtship is a precursor to breeding and begins early in the year. By late winter in quiet northern forests the night air fills with the rhythmic hooting of owls both proclaiming a territory and looking for a mate. While it is the males that are most vocal, females reply and perform musical hooting duets. These strengthen pair bonds and reaffirm the possession of their territory.

Left: This species is strictly
nocturnal but can sometimes be
located roosting during the day
in large tree holes or in ivy.

David Tipling observes:

"Each December a tawny owl comes and calls outside the bedroom window at our house. One year as an owl was calling, another started calling at the back of the property. I thought it was someone playing an owl call as a joke because not only did it sound really loud but this species call is the classic *woo-wuwuwoo* that we have got so used to hearing when watching a creepy scene on TV. This hooting, however, soon descended into a spine-chilling caterwauling as both males competed against each other, clearly there was an interloper in our resident owl's territory. There is something reassuring on hearing the owl call during the long nights of mid-winter. It gives me a sense of hope that spring is a little closer."

Not all owls call at night. The tiny Eurasian pygmy owl produces his single monotonous note – sometimes with an added trill if excited – during daylight hours. Contrasting with the large Eurasian eagle owl, which has a deep far-carrying hoot and which calls most actively on moonlit nights. Other species are quieter on nights such as these because they take advantage of being able to detect prey more effectively. However recent research has shown that eagle owls will seek out high perches from which to call, during which they expose a white flash of feathers on their throat that is visible to other owls under a moonlit sky.

Once pair bonds have been reaffirmed between two birds they then choose a suitable nest site. Owls do not actually build the structure, but use natural holes, tree cavities and old crows or raptor nests, while other species such as the short-eared owl will nest on the ground.

Above: This Eurasian pygmy owl is brooding her chicks in a nest box specially erected in a commercial forestry plantation where no natural nest holes exist.

Top: Short-eared owls lay an egg a day and so hatching is staggered, hence why there are still unhatched eggs in this nest containing very small young.

Above: This picture of the same nest as above shows the youngest owlets at around 10 days old.

Above: The ural owl often ferociously attacks anyone who ventures close to their nest hence they are called *Slaggula* meaning 'attacking owl'.

Opposite: While great grey owls favour large stick nests, both natural and artificially provided structures, they will also readily use broken or burnt tree stumps as pictured here.

Left: A young and still flightless great grey owl has the ability to explore by climbing.

Below: The male great grey owl does all the hunting while the female incubates and then tends to their small young in the nest.

Jari Peltomäki observes:

"In 1992 I moved 500 kilometres north to the Finnish region of Oulu – one of the best places in the world for great grey owls. I remember as if it were yesterday when I found my first great grey owl nest. I entered a beautiful piece of old-growth forest and immediately found some large spruce and aspen trees. I had a strong sense that this was a really exciting place and that I would discover something special, and I did! I found myself looking up into a tall aspen at a huge stick nest once used by a goshawk. A big round owl head was poking out as the bird looked down at me from the top. My blood was running fast. I was completely thrilled.

After this first nest I found numerous others, and altogether, have spent many weeks with breeding great grey owls. During my early encounters, I would ring the owl chicks, but in the last 10 years I have not only photographed them, but have also occasionally fed the birds.

Since the forests close to where I live are commercially harvested, and are generally young trees, there are not many natural nest sites available. I have built many artificial stick nests for great grey owls and they are happy to use them. One year I was in such a hurry to put something up that I placed baskets in the area where there were many birds calling. To my surprise the owls accepted my offerings and started using them instantly.

Over the years we have put up hundreds of nest boxes for owls and have built many artificial stick nests for great grey owls in this area. I'm convinced that this is actually helping the birds because it is providing the owls with nest locations in an area otherwise poor in natural sites. Yet the habitat itself which is a mosaic of forest, fields and clear-cut areas, might actually be better for the owls' key prey species (voles) than extensive old growth forests."

Left: A male snowy owl arrives at the nest with a vole.

Below: A female snowy owl feeds her chick with prey brought to the nest by the male.

Prey availability normally dictates how many eggs an owl will lay. A snowy owl will lay a clutch ranging from two to 14 eggs depending on how plentiful lemmings are. If prey is very scarce they will not nest. If a lemming population has a sudden crash then chicks may starve to death. Jari witnessed just such an occurrence.

Jari Peltomäki observes:

" I have been fortunate enough to visit the snowy owl breeding grounds in Finnish Lapland on several occasions. As a young ornithologist in 1987 I was searching for breeding purple sandpipers. I did not find any, but was surprised to spot a male snowy owl. I followed this 'ghost of the fjells' with my binoculars and was even more amazed when he landed on a small mound next to a female. I had found the first nesting snowy owls in Finnish Lapland since 1974, when it had also been a good Lemming year and hence a lot of snowy owls bred. Both 1987 and 1988 were good breeding years too.

There are no longer frequent lemming years in Lapland since it was another 20 years before snowy owls returned to breed.

Recently 2007 and 2011 have been good lemming years with breeding snowy owls in Finnish Lapland and in Finnmark in Norway.

During these breeding seasons I have spent weeks photographing the secret lives of this high arctic owl at two different locations. I am sure it is not just co-incidence that these breeding areas are exactly the same as those used previously.

My summer 2007 expedition was a true roller coaster – both physically and emotionally! The site was 30 kilometres from the nearest road and during the two week period I walked more than 200 kilometres over rough terrain. That made the trip physically difficult, but it was also emotionally very hard as we reached the owls' breeding area just as the lemming population had crashed – it was sad to see snowy owl nests with dead chicks and deserted nests.

From our base camp I spotted a golden eagle flying low over the fjells with a male snowy owl in close pursuit. What a great photo that would have been! Witnessing this behaviour led us to search that area and again we came across a sad scene. Dead owl chicks of different

ages and unhatched eggs with a couple of fat lemmings on the side of the nest. The male was sitting nearby and he looked very miserable but there was no sign of the female. It was apparent the golden eagle had killed the female, the male did not know how to feed the chicks!

Of the five nests we found, only one pair successfully fledged young that year.

The 2011 expedition was a bit easier. This time the distance to the breeding grounds from the road was only 15 kilometres and we concentrated on photographing one nest in a picturesque location. It was still hard work – since I spent 180 hours in a small hide during those two weeks and there was also a lot of walking involved with this trip too. However, the location was very beautiful with a lot of breeding waders including spotted redshanks, bar-tailed godwits, red-necked phalaropes, and jack snipe.

It has been a privilege to spend time here. There are no other people to spoil the silence of the wilderness."

Top: Snowy owls take a wide variety of food when lemmings are scarce. Here the female is clutching a duckling.

Above: Once the young are big enough the female snowy owl can then help with providing food.

65

Owl eggs are white and round in shape and are laid at intervals by the female, sometimes even a few days apart. Unlike many birds, owls incubate as soon as the first egg is laid resulting in sequential hatching. This means a typical nest will have owlets of varying age and size. In years when there are few voles this means just the strongest chick may survive. If food is in very short supply then the smaller chicks are consumed by their elder siblings, a pattern that is commonplace in large barn owl families.

Certain species are notorious for their aggressive defence of their nest site, as demonstrated by the incident in which Eric Hosking lost his eye to a tawny owl. This is not an isolated event. Owl attacks on people and particularly dogs are reported annually and particularly in Scandinavia. Here both the eagle owl and ural owl will either inflict violent injuries, or will make violent attacks. Ural owls are large residents of the boreal forest and their aggressive nature is underlined by their Swedish name *Slaguggla*, which means 'Attacking Owl'.

By the time the chicks are ready to leave the nest, the build up of decaying prey and general detritus makes quite a stench. While some species attempt to keep the nest clean, others, such as the Eurasian pygmy owl and Tengmalm's owl, are poor housekeepers. Food even starts to accumulate in the nest while the female is incubating the eggs and as her mate keeps her supplied. There are rare occasions, however, when males incubate the eggs or brood the young for a short period.

After two or three weeks, depending on the species, the owlets grow an insulating layer of down called the mesoptile. The chicks' capacity to survive without being brooded allows the female to help the male in feeding them. As the chicks build their strength and acquire the ability to walk and climb they may leave the nest and move short distances. If one should accidentally fall off its perch, by this stage the owlet will be a strong climber and is able to clamber up into trees or bushes out of reach of foxes and other ground predators.

Opposite, left: A young ural owl.

Opposite, right & above: Eurasian eagle owls have a fierce look, even when they're still chicks in the nest.

Left: When looking at this northern hawk owl chick it is easy to see how in Scandinavian folklore such young owls were considered as trolls—human-like beings with evil intent.

Jari Peltomäki observes:

"I have watched and photographed from my hide many hawk owl nests. The chicks leave the nest when they are about three weeks old and, although at that stage, they are unable to fly, they look like little trolls as they walk and clamber around the trees.

Chicks leave the nest in age order, usually one chick per day. Adult birds can be furious defenders of their vulnerable young ones once they are out of the nest and I have to be very careful when approaching my hide, since they attack with lightening speed and often from behind!"

Owls and people

Previous page & above: Traffic accidents are one of the most common causes of mortality in barn owls due to them often hunting along roadside verges.

Opposite: Man-made structures such as church towers offer perfect nesting sites for barn owls.

Right: An ancient Greek four-drachma coin, featuring the little owl.

We know that owls have long held a fascination for people because the earliest cave paintings of them date back about 30,000 years. Sometimes they were viewed simply as a source of food, for others they were associated with witchcraft or linked to ideas of wisdom. But owls constantly recur in folklore throughout the world.

In ancient Egypt an owl glyph, which represented the sound of the letter 'm', appears regularly in that country's hieroglyphic writing. In ancient Greece, however, the little owl was considered sacred to the guardian deity of Athens, Pallas Athene, and even now the little owl's scientific name is *Athene noctua*, meaning 'Athene by night'. The bird was depicted on the city's old four-drachma piece and can be seen on the Greek one-euro coin to this day.

A human-like face has given rise to the owl as a symbol of wisdom. Perhaps it is the humanoid appearance, coupled with their largely nocturnal lifestyle, when they seem to float at the edges of our imagination, that gives them an air of mystery. This in turn, once helped to nurture strongly negative superstitions, as opposed to the more positive associations we have today.

BIRDS OF ILL OMEN.

CHORUS OF FOREIGN JOURNALISTS. "TU-WHIT!—TO-WAR!—TU-WHIT!—TO-WAR!!"
MR. P. "OUT ON YE, OWLS, NOTHING BUT SONGS OF DEATH?"

In central Europe the little owl's sudden bounding appearance and blood curdling calls often heard in the dead of night resulted in its reputation as a bird of death. The owls role as a bringer of bad luck is also a common theme found throughout human folklore. In Britain the barn owl, once known as the screech owl owing to its piercing vocalizations, is often only glimpsed during the hours of darkness as a fleeting and ghostly apparition. It is perhaps no surprise that these unnerving encounters led to the bird being drenched in superstition. Some of the beliefs were so strongly held that

farmers nailed dead barn owls to the barn door with the intention to ward off evil spirits and bad weather.

In some old churches and cathedrals in Britain it is still possible to find misericords (small shelves in the choir stalls, on which monks could lean or sit when they were tired from long periods of standing) where owls have been depicted being mobbed by small birds. Good examples occur in both Norwich and Gloucester Cathedrals. These scenes reflect a medieval belief that the Jews, in their doctrinal rejection of Jesus Christ, were like owls that preferred the darkness to the daylight of the Christian faith. These misericord images of owls being harassed by groups of songbirds also evoked the manner in which individual jews were often attacked by mobs of Christians.

Above: The misericord from Gloucester Cathedral.

Opposite: This cartoon that appeared in *Punch* in January 1888, portrays owls as foreign journalists writing of impending war and so, in the typical stereotype of the time, as bringers of doom. Political manoeuvring in the run-up to the Great War led to many different alliances, including for a short period Germany, Austria and Russia.

Right: A ural owl looks down at the photographer below. Owls have over the centuries, been portrayed both as wise and in some cultures, as foolish too.

Below: There are 'owlaholics' who will collect anything to do with owls...

Such symbolic representations of owls were once widespread, as was the birds' status as an omen of evil. Often the prophecies centred on the home. In France if a pregnant woman heard an owl it would mean her child would be a girl. Another from Ireland held that if an owl ever entered your property, it should be killed at once before it could fly away, so that it would not take the luck of the house with it.

Popular culture has in more recent times pushed these old beliefs aside and embraced the owl in fable and verse. Edward Lear's

nonsense verse *The owl and the pussycat* made a fictional star of the owl. More recently JK Rowling's Harry Potter books have mixed wisdom and witchcraft and made avian celebrities of such species as the snowy owl. Owls have become sporting symbols too, notably in football. The English club, Sheffield Wednesday, after receiving an owl mascot to honor the clubs stadium at Owlerton, became known as the Owls.

In 2007, during a European Championship match between Finland and Belgium, at the national stadium in Helsinki, an eagle owl nicknamed Bubi swooped down on to the pitch causing play to be suspended. Eventually the owl did vacate the arena, but not before it had perched on both sets of goal posts and had thoroughly entertained the whole crowd. From that day, the Finnish team has been known as *Huuhkajat*, which is their name for the Eurasian eagle owl. With typical Finnish humour, Bubi's performance led to him being named Helsinki Citizen of the Year, in December 2007.

Northern owls

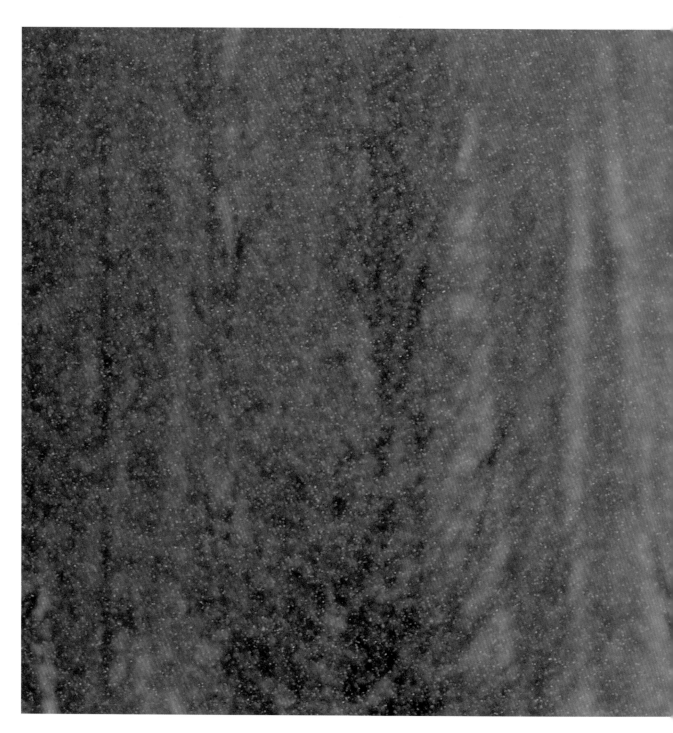

The following accounts give detail on those
12 species of owl living in northern Europe...

Barn owl

Tyto alba

Fact File

Barn owls are susceptible to prolonged cold spells and especially extended snow cover, hence their northern limit is southern Sweden. As a result, populations fluctuate annually. They favour open areas but will hunt in woodland during winter when prey is hard to find.

East Anglia, and in particular the coastal marshes and meadows of North Norfolk in England, is one of the best locations on the planet to watch barn owls. Here they readily hunt during the day in late winter and again in early summer when feeding young.

SIZE: length 29-44cm

CALL: A harsh screech made by both sexes, hence its former name 'screech owl'.

PREY: Mainly voles but will readily take any suitably sized rodent. Hunts from a perch and commonly quarters meadows in silent flight.

BREEDING: Breeds from March. Often nests in barns and outbuildings. Readily takes to nest boxes. Natural nest sites are holes in trees. When prey availability is good barn owls will have two broods, the average clutch size is 4-6 eggs. Eggs are incubated for 32 days and young take up to 62 days to fledge and leave the nest.

Right: A quiet barn is the perfect place to nest and roost.

Opposite: Barn owls hunt in silent flight.

Snowy owl
Bubo scandiacus

Fact File

A highly nomadic species of the far north that only appears to breed during years when lemming populations are high. Snowy owls bred on the Scottish northern isles of Shetland in the late 1960s and early 70s, last breeding in 1975. Wandering individuals appear in Britain, most often on the Western and Northern Isles and often linger for months before moving on.

In Norway, Sweden and Finland perhaps a few hundred pairs may have bred in 2011, which was the first very good breeding year since 1974. Three snowy owls in Norway were fitted with radio transmitters in 2007 revealing movements of thousands of kilometres for each individual as they travelled east to west or vice versa across the Arctic. These nomadic wanderings are undertaken as the birds search for the plentiful food supplies that underpin the species' breeding prospects.

SIZE: length 53-70cm

CALL: A deep resonating hoot of two to six notes. Will make a noise when disturbed that is not unlike a barking dog. Also has a nasal chipping call.

PREY: Lemmings and voles are their primary food source during the summer months. However if food is scarce, birds are readily taken with duck and grouse high on the menu.

BREEDING: Breeds on the Arctic Tundra normally on raised ground so the incubating female can keep an eye out for potential predators such as the Arctic Fox. Nests are defended vigorously.

Males display in a courtship that involves holding their wings in an angel-like posture with their tail cocked while holding a lemming and hooting. Clutch sizes can be as large as 16 eggs, but five to eight is more normal.

Top right: Female snowy owls are speckled, as opposed to the pure white of the male, above.

Eurasian eagle owl

Bubo bubo

Fact File

Eagle owls were once heavily persecuted in Europe, but in some areas they have increased, while in other countries, such as Finland, declines continue. In Britain a small but growing breeding nucleus has developed from escaped bird keepers birds. It is also possible that European immigrants have joined this population, but there is no firm evidence to confirm this. Eagle owls' preferred habitat is open forest and rocky cliffs. They do not shun human habitation and a number of pairs reside in Helsinki and in other European cities.

SIZE: The world's largest owl. Length 58-75cm

CALL: A deep booming *woo-ha* hoot. Males will duet with their mate.

PREY: Eagle owls hunt largely from a static position, watching and waiting, but will also pursue prey in active flight. Quarry includes mammals ranging from mice to hares right up to foxes and small deer. They also eat birds and readily take other birds of prey including all other species of owl that may try to live within their territory.

BREEDING: Eagle owls often pair for life. They nest on cliff ledges, sometimes in quarries, and also on the ground in forests under fallen tree trunks or bushes or in old large disused nests. Up to four eggs are laid at three-day intervals. The female remains in the nest once the young are hatched for around two weeks. Once fledged the young are looked after for another three to four months, before being encouraged to move out of their parents' territory.

Above: This nest was under a fallen tree root.

Left: Eagle owls are formidable predators, capable of taking prey larger than themselves.

Tawny owl

Strix aluco

Fact File

Tawny owls occur in parkland and forests across much of Europe. They extend as far north as central Scandinavia. It is hard to estimate their population size owing to this owl's highly nocturnal, secretive nature.

SIZE: length 36-46cm

CALL: Their call is a drawn-out hoot, a *huhuhuhoo*. A double note *key—ick* is commonly heard too. Often used as a soundtrack for spooky night-time scenes on television.

PREY: Normally hunts from a static position. Takes mostly small animals plus birds, frogs and large insects. Will catch bats in flight.

BREEDING: Tawny owls breed in holes and cavities and take readily to purpose-built nest boxes. They may call at any time of the year but vocalizations reach a peak in mid to late winter. Up to nine eggs are laid from late February. Once the chick hatches, the female broods the chicks for two weeks while the male brings food. A month or so after hatching, the young may leave the nest and sit nearby while still being fed.

Ural owl

Strix uralensis

Fact File

Ural owls reside in old boreal forests and in commercially managed forests if nest boxes are provided. They range across Scandinavia and there some isolated populations further south in Europe. Ural owls are not found in Britain.

SIZE: length 50-60cm

CALL: Various hooting songs but the most common vocalization from the male is a seven-note hooting sequence of two, two and three notes. The female's reply is higher pitched, and she also utters a nasal bark.

PREY: Voles and other rodents, birds, frogs and large insects normally caught from watching and waiting.

BREEDING: Ural owls often pair for life and defend the same territory throughout the year. They nest in tree cavities and holes and use old stick nests. They readily use nest boxes. Unpaired birds will sing from autumn to attract a mate, while paired birds start courting in January when couples can be heard duetting.

Up to six eggs are laid. The female incubates and stays with, or very close to, the young throughout their time in the nest while the male supplies food. Ural owls are notorious for their aggression when they have young. They can ferociously attack any predator or human intruder and can inflict serious injury.

Great grey owl
Strix nebulosa

Fact File

This large grey owl has a head the size of a small child's. They live in the boreal forests of the far north and when food is plentiful stay within the forest. In winter, however, if food is in short supply, great grey owls can be watched hunting in meadows and other open habitats. They range across Scandinavia and can be highly nomadic.

SIZE: length 57-71cm

CALL: The male has a deep hooting sequence in a rhythm reminiscent of the sound produced when using a bicycle pump.

PREY: A vole specialist but they will take other rodents and sometimes birds. Great grey owls hunt either from a perch or will quarter the ground in search of food. They hunt mainly at dawn and dusk, although when feeding young and during winter will hunt during the day.

BREEDING: Males start calling in late winter to attract a mate. Courtship includes mutual preening and offering food.

Great grey owls nest in old stick nests of goshawks or other large birds or sometimes on an old stump close to the ground. They will also use artificial nests including dog baskets! Usually up to six eggs are laid, with the male doing all the hunting while the female incubates and tends the small young. As with many other young owls, they leave the nest before they can fly and walk about in the branches of trees close by. Once they have fledged the adults stay in attendance for another two months.

Opposite, top: The forest edge offers a good vantage point from which to scan for prey.

Opposite: A great grey owl's feet are relatively small compared to other large owls, but their claws are needle-sharp and have a wide reach.

Above: Dog baskets can make the perfect artificial nest platform!

Northern hawk owl

Sturnia ulula

Fact File

A bird of the far northern forests. Hawk owls are fond of open mixed and coniferous forests favouring areas close to clear fell in which they can often be found perched high up on a spruce or other prominent tree. Nomadic in some autumns large numbers of hawk owls may move south in search of food.

SIZE: length 36-42cm

CALL: Male hawk owls have an excited bubbling display call which he also uses when he brings food to the female at the nest. The female answers with a hoarse begging call. They also give a falcon like *kvi-kvi-kvi-kvi* alarm call.

PREY: Hawk owls hunt by watching from a perch. They prey on voles and other rodents and birds taken in flight.

BREEDING: Nests in tree holes and nest boxes and they use abandoned stick nests too. The male starts to advertise his territory from February when he undertakes a wing clapping display flight. Duetting and mutual preening follow. On average up to eight eggs are laid. The male does all the hunting until the chicks are around two weeks old. Once the young have fledged they are tended for another 20-30 days before being fully independent.

Opposite: An owlet dances along
a branch on a summer's evening.

Above: It is the male owl that does most of the hunting during their breeding
cycle, bringing food back to the nest, both for his mate and their chicks.

Eurasian pygmy owl

Glaucidium passerinum

Fact File

Found across central and northern Europe, this fearless little owl is a voracious hunter despite its pocket scale. Pygmy owls favour boreal forests and mountain slopes.

SIZE: length 15-19cm

CALL: Simple one-note whistle uttered every one to two seconds, and when excited, this can speed up into short trills. Very monotonous. The female has a very thin whistle when begging for food from a male. Pygmy owls also have a distinctive call in autumn, an ascending five to seven whistles.

PREY: They hunt largely at dawn and dusk taking birds often larger than themselves plus rodents particularly voles.

BREEDING: Male pygmy owls advertise their presence in late winter by calling from exposed perches. Pygmy owls are hole nesters utilising old woodpecker cavities or nest boxes where these are provided. Active nests can often be identified by the remains of prey piled below the site. Often the male will arrive with prey and call the female off the nest to collect the food. Once the young are old enough to be left unguarded the female departs to undertake her moult, while the male completes the rearing of their brood by himself. Young pygmy owls only leave the nest when able to fly.

Little owl
Athene noctua

Fact File

Little owls stop short of reaching Scandinavia but are found commonly across central Europe and in parts of Britain where they were introduced in the nineteenth century. Typically a bird of open countryside inhabiting woodland edges, wooded hedgerows and around habitation.

SIZE: length 21-23cm

CALL: A long single low-pitched *gooeek* call. Their alarm call is an explosive *chi chi chi*.

PREY: Little owls prey on small birds, amphibians and reptiles such as small snakes and lizards. Also large insects and earthworms.

BREEDING: Pair bonds can last for several years as both sexes reside throughout the year in the same territory. Up to six eggs are laid and the male then provides for the female until the chicks are old enough to be left on their own. They tend to the chicks for a further three to four weeks after fledging.

Right: Little owls are birds of open country, often seen perched low to the ground on boulders or fence posts.

Tengmalm's owl
Aegolius funereus

Fact File

Tengmalm's owl is large headed with a cat-like face. They occur from the northern boreal forests south into central Europe. Tengmalm's owls are nocturnal and difficult to see away from their nests or day-time roost.

This species are susceptible to predation from pine martens and if you scratch the tree trunk to imitate a climbing predator below an active Tengmalm's nest, the female will peer out of their hole with a surprised stare.

SIZE: length 23-28cm

CALL: High pitched five to eight hooting notes that carries farther than most other owl calls. On a still night in a Scandinavian forest the call may travel three to four kilometres or more.

PREY: Feeds mainly on voles and will take birds when vole populations are low.

BREEDING: Nests in tree cavities, such as old black-woodpecker holes, and will use nest boxes in forests where natural holes are absent. Males start to call in early to mid February and once courtship starts they entice females to suitable nest sites for her to inspect. Up to seven eggs are laid and the male then provides for the female and young until she is able to leave the chicks unattended. Once the young have left the nest the male continues to feed them for another few weeks.

Above: Tengmalm's owls have a mildly irritated look when encouraged to peer out from their nest hole or box.

Opposite: Food shortages can encourage Tengmalm's owls to fly long distances of 1,000 kilometres or more. These are known as irruptive movements.

Long-eared owl
Asio otus

Fact File

Long-eared owls are largely nocturnal and one of our more secretive species. They are most easily seen in winter when they often form communal roosts. Even then they can be a challenge to spot as they sit motionless among ivy or tangled branches where they blend perfectly to their surroundings. This species, like the eagle owl, has prominent 'ear' tufts but despite the name, these are not true ears. Their purpose has been hotly debated, but it may be that they simply help break up the owl's outline and increase the bird's camouflage. They reach central Scandinavia but are migratory in the northern part of their range and in Britain the local resident population is joined by wintering migrants from the continent. During autumn these birds can sometimes be seen along the east coast as they arrive off the North Sea.

SIZE: length 35-40cm
CALL: Short hoots repeated every two seconds. Female response is a hoarser but similar hoot.
PREY: Long-eared owls feed largely on voles but also take birds.
BREEDING: Males may start calling in late autumn into early winter if resident. Migrants begin to vocalise in spring when they arrive back from their wintering quarters. Display flights involve the male moving at treetop height when he claps his wings together on the downward stroke. They nest in copses and forests close to more open space in which this species hunts. Old stick nests of raptors, crows or even herons are used and up to eight eggs are laid. The male provides food for the female and chicks until they start to leave the nest at around three weeks after hatching. They are able to fly after a further two weeks.

Top, right: Ear tufts give this owl a cat-like look.

Right: The long-eared owl has an uncanny ability to conceal itself by day.

Short-eared owl

Asio flammeus

Fact File

An open-country owl with a distinctive buoyant flying action. They are found across northern Europe with those in Scandinavia migrating south in autumn. Short-eared owls are one of the more nomadic species of owl and where there are population explosions of voles large numbers of owls may arrive to breed.

SIZE: length 34-42cm

CALL: The male gives a series of deep hoots and audible wing claps when in display flight.

PREY: Hunts from a perch and commonly seen in slow searching flight quartering grassland for voles.

BREEDING: Males perform display flights that include wing clapping. The bird rises high into the sky and slowly proceeds with exaggerated deep wing beats. Short-eared owls nest on the ground laying an average of seven eggs. The female incubates and tends the young on the nest while the male hunts for the family. If food is plentiful once the chicks are independent, a pair may attempt a second brood.

Above: Short-eared owls both rest and nest on the ground.

Below: Short-eared owls have a buoyant, almost butterfly-like flight.

Information and Acknowledgements

INFORMATION

The Hawk and Owl Trust is the UK's leading charity devoted to bird of prey and owl conservation. Visit **hawkandowl.org** to find out more.

The following books in addition to those listed in the bibliography offer further insight into this fascinating family:

Josep del Hoyo. & A Elliott
Handbook of the Birds of the World Vol 5
Lynx Edicions, Barcelona 1999.

Rob Hume & Trevor Boyer
Owls of the World, Dragon's World,
Limpsfield, Surrey 1991

David Chandler
Barn Owl
New Holland Publishers 2011

ACKNOWLEDGEMENTS

We would like to thank Mark Cocker for his ideas knowledge and assistance with our text, and the team at Evans Mitchell Books for bringing this book to fruition. Finally, a big thank you to Darren Westlake for the brilliant design.

BIBLIOGRAPHY

Karel H. Voous
Owls of the Northern Hemisphere
Collins 1988

Heimo Mikkola
Owls of the World A Photographic Guide
Christopher Helm 2012

Marianne Taylor
Owls
Bloomsbury 2012

Desmond Morris
Owl
Reaktion Books Ltd 2009

Mark Cocker & David Tipling
Birds & People
Jonathan Cape 2013

Payne, R.S.
Acoustic location of prey by barn owls (Tyro alba).
J. Exp. Biol. 54, 535-573 (1971)

Opposite: A snowy owl surveys his Arctic wilderness home.

Other Wildlife Monographs titles published by

Evans Mitchell Books

www.embooks.co.uk

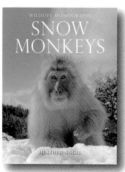

Wildlife Monographs
Snow Monkeys
ISBN: 978-1-901268-37-9

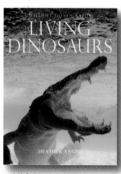

Wildlife Monographs
Living Dinosaurs
ISBN: 978-1-901268-36-2

Wildlife Monographs
Monkeys of the Amazon
ISBN: 978-1-901268-10-2

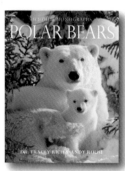

Wildlife Monographs
Polar Bears
ISBN: 978-1-901268-15-7

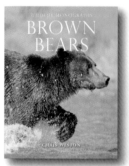

Wildlife Monographs
Brown Bears
ISBN: 978-1-901268-50-8

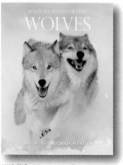

Wildlife Monographs
Wolves
ISBN: 978-1-901268-18-8

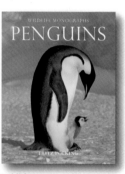

Wildlife Monographs
Penguins
ISBN: 978-1-901268-14-0

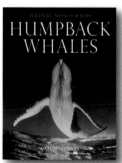

Wildlife Monographs
Humpback Whales
ISBN: 978-1-901268-56-0

Wildlife Monographs
Giant Pandas
ISBN: 978-1-901268-13-3

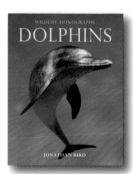

Wildlife Monographs
Dolphins
ISBN: 978-1-901268-17-1

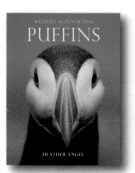

Wildlife Monographs
Puffins
ISBN: 978-1-901268-19-5